D1826487

This Family Reunion

Guest Book

Created
by Stacey Newson

Fathers, Mothers,
Sons and Daughters

Keep In Touch

Family

Together we have everything
If we take the time to be family
Showing love and sharing
Life, stories, linage, and history

E-MAIL

NAME

PHONE

E-MAIL

NAME   PHONE

6

E-MAIL

NAME   PHONE

_____

_____

_____

_____

_____

_____

_____

_____

_____

_____

_____

_____

_____

E-MAIL

NAME

PHONE

E-MAIL

NAME

ADDRESS

E-MAIL

NAME   **ADDRESS**

_____

_____

_____

_____

_____

_____

_____

_____

_____

_____

_____

_____

_____

_____

E-MAIL

NAME

ADDRESS

E-MAIL

NAME

ADDRESS

E-MAIL

NAME

ADDRESS

E-MAIL

NAME   **ADDRESS**

E-MAIL

NAME   ADDRESS

E-MAIL

NAME   ADDRESS

E-MAIL

NAME

ADDRESS

E-MAIL

NAME   **ADDRESS**

E-MAIL

NAME

ADDRESS

E-MAIL

NAME   ADDRESS

E-MAIL

NAME	ADDRESS

E-MAIL

NAME   ADDRESS

_____

_____

_____

_____

_____

_____

_____

_____

_____

_____

_____

_____

_____

E-MAIL

NAME   ADDRESS

_____

_____

_____

_____

_____

_____

_____

_____

_____

_____

_____

_____

_____

_____

E-MAIL

NAME   ADDRESS

E-MAIL

NAME

ADDRESS

E-MAIL

NAME   ADDRESS

E-MAIL

NAME   ADDRESS

_____

_____

_____

_____

_____

_____

_____

_____

_____

_____

_____

_____

_____

E-MAIL

NAME

ADDRESS

E-MAIL

NAME   **ADDRESS**

_____

_____

_____

_____

_____

_____

_____

_____

_____

_____

_____

_____

_____

E-MAIL

NAME   ADDRESS

E-MAIL

NAME   ADDRESS

E-MAIL

NAME   ADDRESS

E-MAIL

NAME   **ADDRESS**

_____

_____

_____

_____

_____

_____

_____

_____

_____

_____

_____

_____

_____

E-MAIL

NAME   ADDRESS

Lightning Source UK Ltd.
Milton Keynes UK
UKIC031337280519
343423UK00006B/284